I am a seal

First published in 2010 by New Holland Publishers (NZ) Ltd
Auckland • Sydney • London • Cape Town

www.newhollandpublishers.co.nz

218 Lake Road, Northcote, Auckland 0627, New Zealand
Unit 1, 66 Gibbes Street, Chatswood, NSW 2067, Australia
86–88 Edgware Road, London W2 2EA, United Kingdom
80 McKenzie Street, Cape Town 8001, South Africa

Barbara Todd has asserted her right to be identified as the author of
this work.

Publishing manager: Christine Thomson
Project management: Wooden Shed, Auckland
Design: Vasanti Unka

National Library of New Zealand Cataloguing-in-Publication Data

Todd, Barbara, 1941-
I am a seal / by Barbara Todd ; illustrated by Helen Taylor.
(I am a-)
ISBN 978-1-86966-287-5
1. Seals (Animals)— Juvenile literature. [1. Seals (Animals)
2. Marine mammals.] I. Taylor, Helen J. (Helen Joy), 1968- II. Title.
III. Series: Todd, Barbara, 1941- I am a-
599.79—dc 22

10 9 8 7 6 5 4 3 2 1

Colour reproduction by Pica Digital Pte Ltd, Singapore
Printed in China through Toppan Leefung Printing Ltd, on paper
sourced from sustainable forests.

Also in this series:

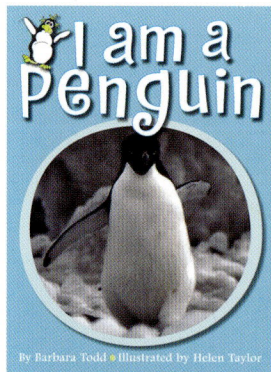

I am a Penguin
ISBN 978 1 86966 246 2

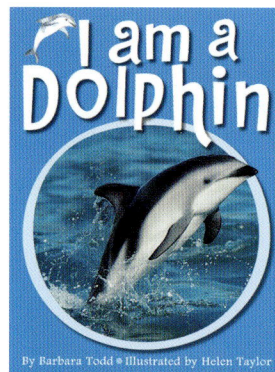

I am a Dolphin
ISBN 978 1 86966 264 6

I am a seal

By Barbara Todd • Illustrated by Helen Taylor

NH
NEW HOLLAND

On the land, in the sea
It's no big deal
They are both home to me
I AM A SEAL!

When I'm resting, the land
Is the best place to be
When I start feeling hungry
I head for the sea

Two flippers in front
And two at the back
Help me swim mighty fast
When I'm chasing a snack

I catch big fish and small fish
Octopus and squid
My two large round eyes
Help me find where they're hid

Sometimes my catch
Is just too big to eat
So I shake it, then toss it
For bite-size seal treats

I give birth to live babies
I have to breathe air
I feed my pups milk
And I'm covered with hair

I'm a mammal, like dolphins
But I'm different, you see
I can climb up on land
Dolphins stay in the sea

Not every seal

Looks exactly the same

Each type of seal

Has its very own name

Ten types are called fur seals

Six types are called sea lions

Eighteen types are true seals
No, I'm not lying!

Fur seals and sea lions
Have small pointy ears

But true seals are earless
Or so it appears ...

I'm a true seal

Look, no ears sticking out!

But check under my hair

You'll find ear holes, no doubt

A true seal's back flippers
Stick straight out behind
So on land I must wiggle
I can't really climb

Some of us live

Where there's thick ice and snow

So we slither and slide

Everywhere that we go

I'm an Elephant Seal
Males have a HUGE nose
Like an elephant's trunk
Hence our name, I suppose

I'm the largest true seal
I sleep quite a lot
And throw sand on my body
When it gets really hot

I'm called a fur seal
I'm covered with hair
And underneath that
I have thick fluffy fur

Each kind of fur seal
Looks almost the same
But we're from different places
And we have different names

New Zealand

Subantarctic

Antarctic

Galápagos

I am a sea lion

I got my fierce name

'Cause the male's neck is hairy

Like a male lion's mane

The boys are enormous
Their voices are LOUD!
The girls are much smaller
And hang out in a crowd

When sea lions and fur seals
Come up onto land
We use all of our flippers
To walk and to stand

Our hind flippers turn forward

We climb without fear

High up on the rocks

We are seal mountaineers!

And flippers are useful
When we have an itch
Five nails on each flipper
Scratch places that twitch

We seals have a problem!

If we're going to survive

We need humans to help us

And keep us alive

STOP DANGER

Please pick up your rubbish

Don't throw nets in the sea

Be careful in boats

And keep an eye out for me!

On the land, in the sea
It's no big deal
We live all round the world
WE ARE ALL SEALS!

Did you know?

• Seals, like whales and dolphins, are known as marine mammals. They breathe air, give birth to live young and nurse their young with milk. They are also warm-blooded. Seals find their food in the sea, but, unlike whales and dolphins, they return to land to mate and give birth.

• Seals belong to a group known as the pinnipeds, which means 'fin-footed'. There are 35 types or species of pinniped.

• Eighteen pinniped species are known as true seals. A true seal has no ear lobes; its ears are just small slits hidden under the thick hair on its head. Also, its rear flippers cannot rotate forward, so the seal does not 'walk' on land. A true seal must move by wriggling its body, sometimes using the front flippers to pull itself along. In the water, a true seal moves its hind flippers to push itself along and its front flippers for steering.

• Sixteen pinniped species are known as eared seals. Ten of these are fur seals, and six are sea lions. An eared seal has ear lobes that you can see. The hind flippers of fur seals and sea lions can rotate forward. They can be used as 'hind feet', enabling the animals to walk, run and even climb when on land. In the water, eared seals use their front flippers for propulsion and their hind flippers for steering.

• The thirty-fifth pinniped species, the Walrus, is very different from the others and is classified separately, so it is not mentioned in this book. It lives in the Arctic.

• All seals are covered with stiff, oily waterproof hair. Fur seals also have a layer of silky underfur next to the skin. All seals have a layer of fatty blubber under the skin, which helps keep them warm.

• Seals are found in every ocean, from polar regions to tropical islands.

• All seals use their eyes, ears and whiskers to help find and catch prey. The eyes see clearly both above and below water, even when there is very little light. Whiskers can feel underwater vibrations created by the movements of fish, squid and tiny crustaceans such as krill.

• Most seals eat fish or squid. Some also feed on krill, while others sometimes take seabirds and even seal pups. Seals do not chew their food. If their catch is too big to be swallowed whole, they break it into smaller pieces.

• In the past, seals were hunted for their fur and oil, some almost to extinction. Today, many populations have recovered, but some are still at risk. They are disturbed at their breeding sites by humans, and an estimated 100,000 seals are killed each year by fishing nets, chemical pollution, plastics and oil spills.

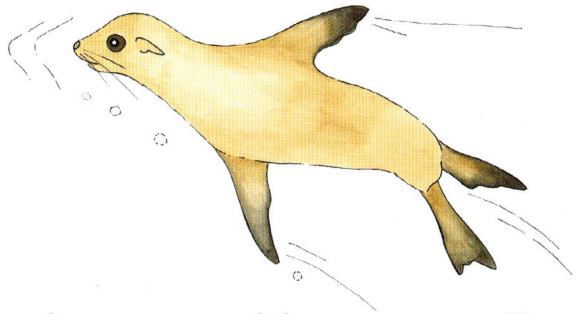

• The New Zealand Sea Lion is one of the rarest sea lions in the world with a population of around 12,000 animals. There was a fifty per cent decline in new pups between 1999 and 2009. Some New Zealand Sea Lions are eaten by sharks, but their greatest danger is from disease and from getting caught in fishing nets.

Teacher/Parent Notes
Try these activities with your children for added learning and lots of fun!

Seals are marine mammals. Talk about the characteristics of mammals (see pg 10 and 30). Compare seals with land mammals, such as dogs and cats, and with other marine mammals, such as whales and dolphins. See if the children can discover other mammals that use both the land and sea, such as otters and polar bears. What physical features do they have in common with seals?

A seal's body is like a living thermos flask: blubber beneath the skin works like insulation to maintain a constant body temperature of about 38.5 °C. (That's just warmer than ours.) In the morning, fill a plastic bottle and a thermos flask with hot water, then set them aside. Have the children check them each hour and compare the temperatures of the two. A seal's blubber also helps keep it cool, so you could do the same experiment with iced water.

Seals have their own natural 'raincoats'! A seal's body is covered with stiff, oily hair that helps keep its skin dry. Find a piece of wood – cork works really well – and have children pour water on it. The wood gets wet and absorbs some of the water. Next, have them brush cooking oil on the wood, and then pour water over it. What happens? Experiment with other materials, or different types of oil.

True seals use only their front flippers to help them move on land. Try moving like a true seal by wriggling your body over the floor, by hunching up and straightening out, or by pulling yourself along with your front 'flippers'. Are there other ways you can move without using your 'back flippers'?

Seals breed in colonies, or rookeries, and at times there may be dozens of pups all together. The pups look very alike, so how do mums tell them apart? Each pup has its own smell and its own tone of voice. (Seals give a high-pitched bark, rather like that of a dog.) When a mum returns from fishing at sea, she calls to her pup and listens for its reply; she can then go to nurse it. Pick one child to be a 'mum' and have the other children act as 'pups' sitting in a circle around her. Have the mum pick out one child to be her pup and listen to its 'bark'. Then blindfold the mum and turn her to face one of the pups. She 'barks' at the pup and listens to its reply. Is it her pup? Keep going around the circle until the mum recognises her own pup. Next, have the mum listen again to her own pup, then blindfold her and have two pups bark at once. She must then try to turn to face her own pup. Keep adding other pups until all the pups are barking at once. Discuss how much harder it is to find your own pup when there are a lot of barking pups around.